Naomi Foyle

Grace of the Gamblers
A Chantilly Chantey

With illustrations by Peter Griffiths

First published in 2010
by Waterloo Press (Hove)
95 Wick Hall
Furze Hill
Hove BN3 1NG

Printed in Palatino 11pt by
One Digital
54 Hollingdean Road
East Sussex BN2 4AA

A CIP record for this book is available
from the British Library

ISBN 978-1-906742-17-1

Acknowledgements

A CD version of Naomi Foyle reciting 'Grace of the Gamblers', recorded by Richard Miles, is available with *Interfaces of the Oral, the Written, and Other Verbal Media*, an anthology of essays edited by Susan Gingell and Wendy Roy (Wilfred Laurier Press, 2010).

A doctoral fellowship from the Arts and Humanities Research Council helped support the writing of this poem under the Bardic supervision of Prof Carol Rumens at Bangor University.

Kevin McGimpsey and John O'Donoghue gave freely of their time to advise me on Irish history and terminology. All errors of fact and judgement are my own.

I am also grateful to Alan Morrison for his sharp editorial eye; Carmel Walsh and Aisling Hillary for their musical contribution to the CD; Bernadette Cremin and Bridget Whelan for their performance of the poem at the launch, and hopefully beyond; Richard Miles for his iron-clad commitment to the Live Literature project; the Limerick City Cuisle International Poetry Festival (2006) for the invitation to West Ireland; Maude Casey for the gold and silver apples of her storytelling; and Paul van Gelder for the seven rainbows walk along the cliffs of Moher.

By the same author

Hush: An Opera In Two Bestial Acts
(Theatre Passe Muraille, Toronto, 1990)

Febrifugue (Treeplantsink Press, 1996)
Red Hot & Bothered (Lansdowne Press, 2003)
Canada (Echo Room Press, 2005)
The Night Pavilion (Waterloo Press, 2008)

Contents

For Mary Griffiths —
Artist, Historian and Beloved Aunt of Many Travels

O come to the convent, young ladies of Mayo,
    We'll arm you with needles and thread.
Outside in the trenches, a summer of spuds
    Is rotting away like the dead…
                                        in their beds …
    Is rotting away like the dead.

Along the grey sands, an ocean is foaming
    Like spit on the lips of the starved.
But girls who can stitch white lace in fine patterns
    Will be fatter than cows due to calve.
                                        To carve!
    Fatter than cows due to calve.

And when you are working your edgings and sprigs,
    Spinning your bobbins and nets,
Remember you're not the first canny colleens
    To unravel the Englishman's threats.
                                        Don't forget
    To unravel the Englishman's threats.

For this is the ballad of Gráinne Ní Mháille,
    Queen of the West Irish Coast.
At ten years of age she hacked off her hair
    And blazoned the air with a boast:

'Me Ma must let me set sail to Spain,
    For I am me father's daughter.
One day I'll captain his galleys and men
    And govern the stormiest water.'

The old fella guffawed, took her aboard,
  Glad of a girl with gumption;
Under his wing she studied the stars,
  The tides and perfect presumption.

For Pa was a chieftain, his hard-won crown
  A silver sea studded with islets,
And if Gráinne could swagger on deck like a man,
  She'd be after commanding his pirates.

Wind at her neck, salt on her lips,
  The crop-headed lassie in britches
Grew into a woman named Granuaile,
  Intent on increasing her riches —

Galley bellies groaning with goods,
  Spare cutlasses stashed in the flax,
In between bartering wool for wine,
  She was rifling wrecks on the rocks!

But a good Gaelic girl must marry and mother,
  The womb is a powerful smithy —
When Granuaile wed an O'Flaherty man
  The whiskey it flowed like the Liffey.

She bore him three tiddlers, collected his rents,
  Defended his land with her vessels;
But Donal, that eejit, died in an ambush,
  Leaving her trapped in Cock's Castle.

O Granuaile's story is shaping up swell,
    Like a river of Limerick lace,
It toiles and billows, tumbles and sprays,
    Til history's calling her Grace.
                              Her Grace…
    Now history's calling her Grace.

And if you can sing as you stitch and you hook
    You'll pin a long tale to your kin,
How a 'femynyne spoiler' battled an empire
    With more than a fortune to win.
                              To spin!
    With more than a fortune to win.

The English were slinging a battering ram,
    The siege was a test of her mettle —
Grace melted the roof, poured hot lead on their heads,
    Cried: 'Call me the Queen of Hen's Castle!'

The O'Flaherty clan said 'Thanks, now scram.
    No widow's got rights to our land.'
Grace sailed back to Mayo with two hundred men,
    To gee up her own bandit band.

Grace of the Gamblers, wanton and bold,
    Played a powerful game in the straits:
If you wanted to sail to Galway City,
    You had to pay Gráinne her rates!

But a woman alone, no matter how stout,
    Was legally all in a pickle:
When Granuaile wedded Iron Richard Bourke,
    'Twas not just for the sake of his prickle.

Some say she divorced him after a year,
    But blood roars louder than rumours:
Gráinne gave birth to his son on a ship
    Being boarded by Turkish corsairs.

The crew came a-crying, so swapping her babby
    For a beltful of black blunderbusses,
She capered on deck like a mad giantess
    And blasted the Barbary bastards.

Tibbot-ne-long grew up to out-shine
    His brothers Murrough and Owen:
When Granuaile gave them a seed each to plant
    The bigger boys dug up a mountain —

But Tibbot's blue eyes, bright as the sky,
    Sought the most fertile soil in all Erin:
When he tossed his seed in the wild Irish sea,
    Hailed Granuaile: 'You are my son.'

O Gráinne's story doesn't end here
    At a moment of motherly love.
Husbands or sons, no man could outdo her
    When Saxon stick came to shove …
                                    Meet the Guv!
    Yes, Saxon stick came to shove.

Bess's new Governor, Sir Richard Bingham,
    Was roping the chieftains in line,
But like a scutched hank of river-ret hemp
    Granuaile twisted and twined …
                                    and twined…
    Granuaile twisted and twined

The Earl of Desmond thought it was cute
    To deliver Ní Mháille to Dublin.
She haggled her freedom, legged it to Mayo,
    And declined to support his rebellion.

Bingham the Brutal set fire to Munster,
    Sealing his fame with a famine.
Thinner than wood smoke, the kerns that survived
    Were fighting the flies for the carrion.

Desmond was gnawing skeletal hopes,
  Pinned his dreams to a fleet of Italians.
Alas, the Pope's soldiers surrendered to Bingham —
  And were slaughtered like so many vermin.

The chieftains took heed, did deals with the Crown,
  Knee-bending on blood-mudded ground.
Now Iron Richard Bourke was a laudy daw 'Sir',
  And Gráinne was sound as a pound.

But Richard fell ill, a savage bad dose,
  Was dead in his bed-shirt by April.
Lickety-split, Old Billygoat Bingham
  Was gumming for the widow of Mayo.

Slavering shite, he inveigled her son
  On to an island at night,
Then hanged eighteen men, strapped Owen down
  And stabbed him twelve times in the throat.

'That poisonous hoor!' Granuaile swore,
  'Will die for his desperate deceits!'
Drawing down gallowglass, Redshanks and muskets,
  She garnered an army of Scots.

Cold-Blooded Bingham circled and swooped
  Down on his prey like a hawk…
When he scooped up a hen for his new gallow-tree,
  She sure wasn't having a lark!

But Granuaile's story won't stop with a squawk,
  Caught in a short, shrinking loop,
For Gráinne the wrangling, roaming sea-captain,
  Could unpick a noose with one whoop.
                              One whoop!
  Could unpick a noose with one whoop.

And if you young ladies would feed your Great Hunger
  With more than shamrocks and cress,
Then stitch a lace sampler of Gráinne's example:
  'Bite the Hand, Break the Bank, Ne'er Confess!'
                              Confess?
  Bite the Hand, Break the Bank, Ne'er Confess!

The best of the Bourkes dangled and swayed,
  Their latest rebellion snaffled;
The thread of her own life bitten and frayed
  Granuaile mounted the scaffold.

To creak of the plank and chafe of the rope,
   She was greeting the gape of her grave —
When a horseman arrived at a nick-o'-time gallop:
   The 'nurse of insurgents' was saved!

So did Grace's nephew, the Devil's Hook,
   Flatter the Pale to deceive?
Or was the white hand of a wily old Tudor
   Behind that vellum reprieve?

The Spanish Armada was flapping its flags
   And `tisn't so hard to believe
That Gráinne might guard the Gaelic back door,
   A trick up Elizabeth's sleeve.

For the sea-faring She-Cock feathered her nest
   With treasure from Skye to Gibraltar;
'Sir Drake? A right quack,' she cackled and spat,
   'My eyes are the best on the water!'

If Liz took the long view and Gráinne the short,
   Preserving her life for a price,
Both of the century's hot-headed queens
   Might survive the next roll of the dice…

Bingham was fuming, deprived of his prize,
   But soon he'd be rooting for more —
Like rheumy old cattle savaged by dogs
   The Armada smashed up on the shore.

Blinder than maggots, flushed out of flesh,
    The Spanish had no time to blink:
Grace killed the fellas wrecked on Clare Island,
    And Bing flung the rest in the brink.

O Granuaile's story spins thicker here,
    In a whirlpool of pillage and spite.
Was she a *sleeveen*, in league with the Queen?
    Or just picking and choosing her fights?
                    That's right!
    She was picking and choosing her fights.

And if you'd unpick the motives of pirates,
    Be ready for blisters and blood:
Gráinne was steely, Gráinne was coarse,
    Not a-feared to be smeared in mud.
                  M'Lud!
    Not a-feared to be smeared in mud…

Though hiding or helping Spanish survivors
    Broke every law of the Saxon,
Some of the chieftains took to harbouring crews,
    And kindly repairing their galleons —

Catching the hint of a chance once again
    To heartily hammer the clans,
Bingham the Lizard stealthily slithered
    Into some shameless shenanigans.

Not happy with skewering two thousand Spaniards,
  The villain declared open season —
He marched into Mayo, up to Granuaile's gate,
  Accusing her nephew of treason.

'Take one more step and I'll hack off your head,'
  Hissed Grace as she paced in the garden.
Bingham of Bloodbath strode down to the village
  And massacred women and children.

Ignited, united, the O'Malleys rampaged
  With Bourkes, Clangibbons and Scots,
Sacking and looting from Arran to Galway,
  Dispatching their powder and shot.

Counting her coppers, shillings and groats,
  The Gingernut stuck in her oar:
Bess ordered Bingham to quit his knick-knacking,
  Take stock of the cost of the war!

Now the chieftains, with all of their millie up muscle,
    Should've given the Guv'nor the oust.
But instead of demanding his instant dismissal
    They foostered and festered and groused.

Soon they were rucking each other and Bingham
    Over various terms and conditions.
Even young Murrough had a mind to submit
    To further his private ambitions.

O Gráinne's beheading her son's closest chums,
    She's burning his buildings, ha ha!
Yes, when Murrough bowed down just one inch to the Crown,
    His gicker got whipped by his Ma.
                                    O Murrough!
    Your gicker got whipped by your Ma!

But here's where the scourge of Mayo is combed
    Into flittering, fluttering strands —
And if bony young ladies would braid the crack back,
    You must iron your bonny green ribands.
                                    Green ribands…
    You must iron your bonny green ribands.

The day the Blind Abbot was shot in a skirmish
    Most of the Bourkes bit the dust.
Soon only Gráinne and Tibbot-ne-long
    Were left to combust in disgust.

When Tibbot hooked up with Red Hugh O'Donnell
    Both boys were using their noggins:
Hugh was a man from a clan with a plan
    Involving Iberian guns.

But the Spanish stayed home and Bingham fought on
    With compasses, plotters and maps.
Charting the rivers and islands of Mayo,
    He drew up some fine pirate traps.

O the mast of the Gaels was struck at the root:
    Tibbot was cruelly taxed,
Red Hugh surrendered to buy up some time,
    And Gráinne slipped under the axe.

Grace of the Gamblers became a mad scrambler,
    Stripped of her dearest possessions;
Bingham impounded her cattle and galleys,
    Destroying her very professions.

Tibbot was soon in the same battered boat,
    A penniless punk in the hold —
But Bingham forgot to cut off her balls,
    And Gráinne neglected to fold!

Her ship was aground, the house held the aces,
    But you can't stop an old vigilante;
'Dry your arse,' she commanded Tibbot-ne-long,
    'Mammy will soon up the ante.'

Instead of a sword, she sharpened a quill
    And flourished her very best Latin:
Stacking a letter with queenly complaints,
    She blackjacked Red Bessie in London!

Oh Granuaile's story gets gauzy right here,
    Veiled by myth appliqué
But the fact that she stitched up a visit to England
    No-one could rightly gainsay.
                                    Ah nay,
    No-one could rightly gainsay.

And if clever young ladies would treat the plain truth
    As if 'twere a priceless material,
You'd nip, slip and tuck, and stretch it a little
    So the bias would flow magisterial.
                                    Imperial?
    O the bias it flows, immaterial…

History vouches that letter found favour,
    As Lizzie's own seal does attest,
And those would read the Pirate's Petition
    May look in the Crown's Treasure Chest.

But Granuaile's pleas — for protection, a pension,
    And permission to slay England's foes —
Cloak her intentions with eloquent guile
    Like a fabric that shimmers and glows.

In her sixty-third summer, Grace sailed to London,
    A city that stank of the plague.
Bessie was off burning herbs in the shires,
    Her diary Royally vague.

[13]

At last an appointment was granted at Greenwich,
    Grace chose her apparel with care –
'Twas well to look regal, yet humble and grateful
    To Her-with-the-pearls-in-Her-hair.

The documents prove the Queen listened with interest
    To the Sea-Madam's story of woe,
In respect of her age, and most dutiful manner
    Considered the case of the widow.

What is not writ is the wit that zig-zagged
    Between these two dagger-bright women.
Thus it has fallen to nights round the peat
    To embroider, to spark, and illumine.

And so it is said that when Gráinne took snuff
    Elizabeth gave her a hanky —
Not cotton or flannel, or the insult of linen,
    But a lacy thing, scented and swanky.

Grace emptied her nose, a victorious blow,
    Then tossed the wet rag in the fire.
The courtiers froze, examined their toes:
    Would Gráinne be next on the pyre?

O Granuaile's story is hotting up here,
    Like a needle tip stuck in a flame.
Would she burn to a cinder by sovereign order?
    Or stick it out till the end of the game?
                     The game…
    Was to last to the end of the game!

So if you are told to make lace through the evening
    But your poor tummy grumbles at dusk,
Lean into the night, and take a deep whiff
    Of Granuaile's growling musk.
                            Her-r-r musk …
    G-r-r-ranuaile's gr-r-rowling musk.

'Is Her Majesty's gift not to your liking?'
    A nobleman stiffly inquired.
'In Erin,' said Grace, 'when a hanky is schnuttered,
    We consider it duly expired.

I would no more bundle my snot in my pocket
    As wash my face in a bog.'
The silence that followed was shattered by laughter:
    Bess nearly fell off her high hog!

Gráinne left London with a fleet of new galleys
    And a letter for Bingham and Co.
Pointing her prow toward emerald shores
    The old hen was beginning to crow.

For the Queen had promised Gráinne a pension
    To be counted from English coffers.
Would Grace soon be back in the thick of the rebels,
    Making them secretive offers?

No, Bess's largesse was only as handsome
    As the clerics who sat on her cash:
And Bingham was gnarly and rank as a dragon
    When it came to protecting his stash.

All through the last petty years of his reign,
    He never gave Gráinne a penny.
'Feck youse!' she scoffed, 'I'll plunder the place
    From Wexford to wee Letterkenny.'

But the Age of the Gaels was sputtering out,
    Despite the three mutinous Hughs:
Their Nine Years' Rebellion ended in exile,
    And for Gráinne and Tibbot, bad news.

Red Hugh O'Donnell sore fancied their land,
    But to reef him meant helping the Crown.
Grace of the Gamblers was forced to flee Mayo,
    The chips and the ships were all down.

O Granuaile's story could hereby dissolve
    Like a boat that sets sail in the mist:
Nobody knows how, when or where
    She knocked out her last game of whist.
                            With her fist!
   She knocked out her last game of whist.

But fear not, famished ladies, for legend supplies
    A well-tailored end to her tale:
Gráinne's bones, it is said, were dug up and ground
    Into meal to feed to the soil.
                         Her soul…
   Was a meal to feed to the soil.

And if a farmer near Glasgow, munching a turnip
    Should fatally choke on her tooth,
It serves Scotland right for joining the Union,
    So what if it isn't the truth!
                         The truth?
   You must dig deep to needle the truth!

Notes

Gráinne Ní Mháille [GRAWN-ya NEE WYL-ya] (1532-1603?), known in English as Grace O'Malley, was the daughter of a chieftain of the Uí Mháille seafaring dynasty on the west coast of Ireland, now County Mayo. Her nickname Granuaile, meaning 'crop-headed', derives from her hair-cut as a child. Young Gráinne showed far more aptitude for sailing than her brother, and eventually succeeded her father as chieftain. For over forty years she owned a fleet of twenty galleys, leading two hundred men in continual raiding, inter-clan warfare and battles with the British. During this period the Tudors were consolidating English control of Ireland by means of crop-burning, famine, massacres, and a political policy of 'surrender and submit'. Chieftains who relinquished their lands and ancestral rights would be re-granted their estates under English laws and titles — but while she could be a sophisticated diplomat in her own defence, and is sometimes suspected of spying for the British, Grace never publicly bent her knee to the Crown.

Twice-married and the mother of four children, Grace maintained political independence from her husbands, and played a dominant role in the fortunes of her three sons. She was unafraid of single combat, fought with cutlass and blunderbuss at sea and on land, and could proudly state that no man under her ever mutinied. How many men were 'under her' is a matter of legend. But though it is largely thanks to folklore, song and poetry that Granuaile has become a heroic Irish figure, the facts of her life are well-documented in the State Papers of both Ireland and England. Amongst other epithets, these historical accounts refer to Grany O'Male as 'a great spoiler, chief commander and director of thieves', and the 'nurse of all rebellions' in her province. Their detailed descriptions of her deeds provide the basis for the two recent biographies that have informed my 'epic ballad' about a powerful and complex female leader. For the iconoclastic Gráinne Ní Mháille was not only a sea captain, pirate and gambler; but a guerrilla fighter defending her land and culture against colonial invasion; and a pragmatic chieftain set on survival in a turbulent age.

Glossary

cute: clever
flitters: tattered and torn
foostering: wasting time
Gallowglass (*galloglaigh*): Scottish forces allied to Irish clans, who came over during the fighting season to help the chieftains fight the English.
gicker: bum
gumming for: salivating, dying for something.
hoor: all-purpose word, usually masculine, meaning someone you disapprove of. (*cute hoor* implies cunning and deviousness, usually applied to politicians.)
kern: Irish common soldier
knick-knacking: knocking on a door then running away.
millie up: a fight's about to start!
The Pale: Dublin and surrounds, controlled in the sixteenth century by the English.
Redshanks: Scottish mercenaries, owing no allegiance to Irish clans, but hired on short-term contracts. According to Judith Cook, they wore leggings made of red deerskin, and are also said to have crossed rivers in the winter, making their legs red.
rooting: searching
to reef: beat a person up
sleeveen: a sly person

Further Reading

Chambers, Anne (1998). *Granuaile, Ireland's Pirate Queen.*
     Dublin, Wolfhound Press.

Cook, Judith (2004). *Pirate Queen: The Life of Grace O'Malley.*
     Cork, Mercier Press.

Dugaw, Dianne. (1989) *Warrior Women and Popular Balladry.*
     Cambridge, Cambridge University Press.

Foyle, Naomi. 'The Ballad As Site Of Rebellion: Orality,
     Gender and the Granuaile Aislingi'. *Interfaces of the Oral,
     the Written, and Other Verbal Media.* Ed. Susan Gingell and
     Wendy Roy. Waterloo, Ontario: Wilfred Laurier Press, 2010.

www.irishslang.co.za